LEWIS WICKES HINE
1874–1940

Teacher, photographer, and champion of children everywhere,
Lewis Hine traveled around the United States in the early
twentieth century, taking pictures of children working under
harsh conditions. His photographs attracted national attention
and assisted in the passage of child labor laws.

There are two things I wanted to do.
I wanted to show the things that had to be corrected;
I wanted to show the things that had to be appreciated.

—Lewis Hine, 1939

The Traveling Camera

Lewis Hine and the Fight to End Child Labor

By Alexandra S. D. Hinrichs

Illustrated by Michael Garland

Getty Publications, Los Angeles

If I could tell the story
in words
I wouldn't need to lug
a camera.

But a picture speaks
its own language,
one most folks,
young and old,
understand.

A picture tells
a big story
in a small space,
can shine light
in a shadowed place.

So I carry a camera,
   a heavy load
      for a featherweight
         to tote,
and my camera
carries hope.

My pictures tell the story
of children laboring
in fields,
    factories,
      mines,
        mills,
          and city streets.

I want to show their hard work,
their hard lives,
to start
people thinking,
to spark
a desire to help,
to ignite
change.

I aim to show
something else, too.

Their spirit. Because
    the human spirit
    is the big thing
    after all.

Come out with me
to one of these canneries
at three o'clock some morning.

The whistle blows. Inside
the shucking shed,
   boys and girls,
   six, seven, and eight years old,
   take their places.

Manuel,
the smallest of the bunch,
stands tiptoe
on a wooden crate.

Little fingers
pry open
sharp oyster shells,
drop the meat into a pot—
    reach
       pry
          drop
            reach
               pry
                  drop
until the pot is full.

Outside
in the cold, damp, dark,
the shell piles grow
   minute upon minute,
   hour upon hour,
   day upon day,
   month after month.

From the cannery
to the cranberry bog.

*At first
the morning is fresh,
and nature
full of beauty.*

Mellie watches
Ma and Pa and
big sister Millie
gather glistening berries.
The family needs as many hands
for as many pennies
as possible.

Millie picks
        picks
            picks
back bent
all day,
straightening only for a hasty haul
to the Bushel Man,
'til the sun begins to scorch,
and any fun in the task
shrivels.

I turn to leave,
feel a tug on my sleeve.
Mellie asks me to take
a picture
of her dolly.

Now come visit the shoe factory.
Hear the factory bell?
Girls and boys
file through the door,
and I follow.

Or I try.
A fist shakes, and a man barks,
"Keep out!"

Well, I'm no fool.
Out I keep.
And I wait.

At noon the bell rings,
the door bangs open.
Charlie and Willie burst through.
Harry halts to hold the door.
    Whatta pal!

Eva and Odella rush past him.
Lunch, and a taste of freedom,
before, all too soon,
the bell calls them back
to whatever it is
the Boss Man
doesn't want me to see.

Next time, I'm ready for
sneak work.

A pad and pencil
are in my pocket
for scribbling one-handed notes
in secret.

I'm fixing to write down
facts
so people will believe
what their eyes don't want to see.

I've measured from the floor to
each button on my coat
to reckon heights and ages.

I've invented a
  waterproof nonsinkable reason
  in advance
  to outwit the guardians
  I am up against.

At the cotton mill,
I tell the overseer
The Company sent me
to take pictures of broken machinery.

He believes me,
lets me inside.

Rows of bobbins whir.
Cotton fluff coats the ground,
floats through the air,
lands in the hair
of the girl before me —
Hattie, three buttons tall.

I ask, "How old are you?"
A pause.
    "I don't remember."
Softer now, a hush in her voice,
    *"I'm not old enough to work,
    but I do just the same."*

There's a heap more kids here
than in the school nearby.
They can't spell their own names.
It's a wonder they can count
the fifty cents they earn
each day.

Over here, outside the mine,
coal and coughs rattle.
Dust chokes the breaker boys
who perch on wood planks,
sorting out slate and stone.

*The coal is always moving
and clattering
and cuts their fingers.*

Their backs ache,
their lungs ache,
and if they fall...
they cannot fall.

Deep inside the coal mine's belly
darkness swallows me whole.
Only my camera can see
for a flash pan's split second.
Yet here Vance sits ten hours a day,
waiting and waiting.

When he hears a coal car's
clunking approach,
he opens the door,
lets the car through,
then waits some more.
It's a dreary life for a fella,
with nothing and nobody for company.

Up and down city streets,
shoppers and diners
waltz around
newsies, bootblacks, and peanut sellers
without missing a beat.

I spy Joseph,
seven years old
and only two buttons tall.

"Extra! Extra! Read all about it!"

His singsong voice jingles
like the coins he dreams of spending
on candy and a moving picture.

An orange in the gutter
not a stone's throw away
will have to do for his supper.

Midnight looms.
Up again and at 'em!

The messenger boys
are just getting started.

*Stanley is afraid
to be out on the street
alone at night.*

So his brother Louis,
who's worked a whole day
already, sticks by him.

Stanley is a rookie.
He doesn't yet know all the streets,
alleys, and corners of the night.
But he knows enough
to keep his eyes peeled
for potholes, motorcars,
and strangers.

They are darn good eggs, these brothers,
earning a couple o' bucks
to help their widowed mother.

Graveyard shift at the glass factory.
Furnaces glow like dragon fire,
and just as hot, too.

Howard runs, not for play,
but to get that bottle into the oven
pronto,
carrying molten glass
at breakneck pace.

He's paid by the piece—
    don't-drop-it
    don't-drop-it
    don't-drop-it.

*Three years in the Glass House
and no chance for promotion yet.*

Howard's shift ends at three in the morning.
He has a crying need for sleep, but
the trolley home won't run 'til six.
He curls up in a corner
and shuts his eyes.

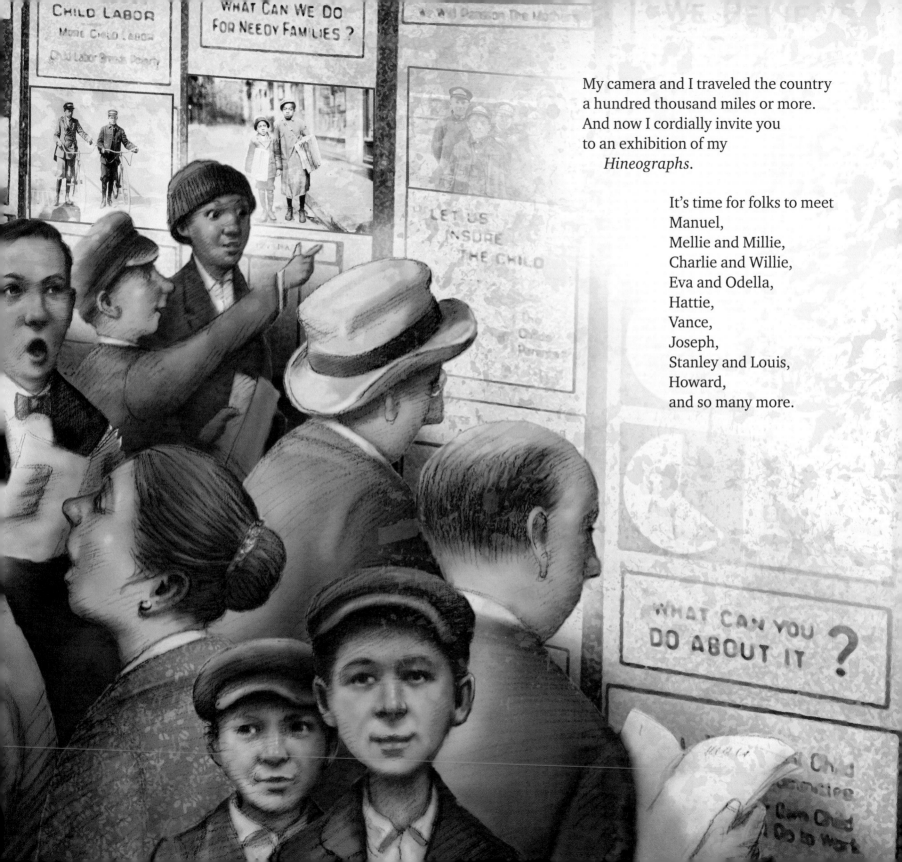

My camera and I traveled the country
a hundred thousand miles or more.
And now I cordially invite you
to an exhibition of my
    Hineographs.

    It's time for folks to meet
    Manuel,
    Mellie and Millie,
    Charlie and Willie,
    Eva and Odella,
    Hattie,
    Vance,
    Joseph,
    Stanley and Louis,
    Howard,
    and so many more.

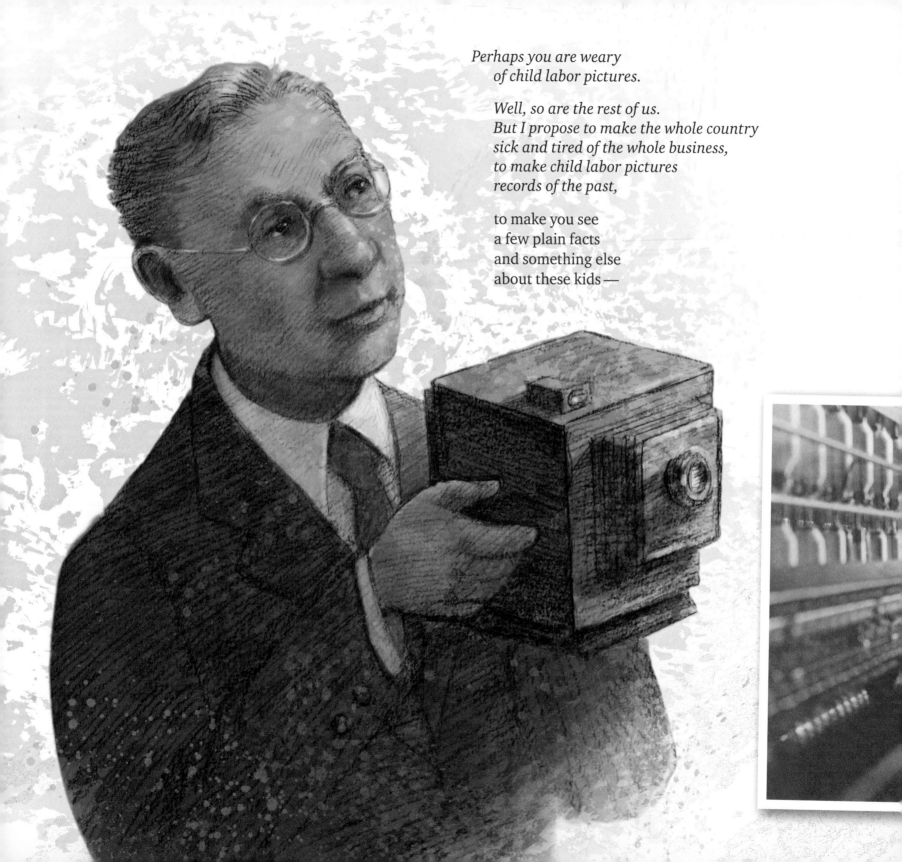

*Perhaps you are weary
of child labor pictures.*

*Well, so are the rest of us.
But I propose to make the whole country
sick and tired of the whole business,
to make child labor pictures
records of the past,*

*to make you see
a few plain facts
and something else
about these kids—*

Their spirit.
That's the big thing after all.

Note to the Reader

The Voice of Lewis Hine

Lewis Hine was a real person with a poetic voice and a great sense of humor. For this book, I wanted him to be the one telling the story. I invented some of his words, basing them on his many letters, reports, and photo captions. Words written by Lewis himself appear in *italics*.

Fact and Fiction

The characters in this story are based on real children who were photographed by Lewis Hine. Some of their names were changed, and sometimes their actions were combined with those of other children Lewis met. In all cases, the fusion of history and storytelling is grounded in careful research.

Lewis Hine and Child Labor

In 1908 Lewis Hine was hired by the National Child Labor Committee (NCLC) to take pictures of children at work. Although kids had helped their parents in family businesses and on farms before, new machines and factories made work even more tedious and dangerous. Children earned low pay, missed school, or worked such late hours they couldn't stay awake in

class. Employers hired children because they were cheaper than adult workers, easier to boss around, and less likely to strike. Some parents might not have wanted their kids to work, but often families needed money for food and housing.

Most people weren't aware of how many kids were working or how bad the conditions really were. Some states had laws about how old children had to be and the hours they could work, but those laws were rarely enforced. Lewis thought

that if people could *see* the children working, it might spur Americans to demand change. He traveled the country, taking pictures and detailed notes, including names and ages. He interviewed children, employers, family members, and teachers. He sometimes disguised himself to sneak into factories, mines, mills, and fields. He pretended to be a Bible salesman, or a postcard salesman, or a photographer taking pictures of the machinery. He traveled with a witness to strengthen his claims. Lewis took thousands of photographs, which were published in magazines, books, and pamphlets and shown at exhibitions. As a result, more states passed or improved laws to limit child labor, to enable more children to go to school, to raise the ages at which they could work, and to improve workplace conditions. Eventually, federal child labor laws were passed.

Child Labor Today

Sadly, child labor continues around the world today. In 2016, an estimated 152 million children were working across the globe—48 percent between the ages of five and eleven, and 71 percent employed in agriculture. Reporters are continuing to investigate the role of child workers in the making of chocolate and palm oil, for example. Times of economic hardship increase the rates of child labor. As I write this in 2020, the COVID-19 pandemic has forced more children and teens to work because their parents are sick or have lost their jobs. Some of these youths have dropped out of school to work full-time to

help their families. Before the pandemic, the United Nations General Assembly had declared 2021 the "International Year for the Elimination of Child Labor."

Lewis Hine and Photography

You have probably seen many pictures of yourself, family, and friends. You may even take your own photos using the tiny cameras in mobile phones. These devices are very different from the cameras of the early 1900s. Lewis's camera was big and required about fifty pounds of equipment. His early pictures were taken with a box-type camera, a bulb shutter, glass-plate negatives, magnesium flash powder, and a wooden tripod ("flimsy and unreliable in a pinch"). To take a

ABOVE: Lewis using a box camera to photograph children near tenement housing, 1906–7.

RIGHT: *Boys Working at an Integrated Glass Factory, Alexandria, Virginia, 1911.*

picture, he first had to decide if he wanted a vertical or horizontal shot; a horizontal one meant that he had to unscrew the box and turn the entire camera on its side. He focused the lens and prepared the flash pan. Finally, if his subject had stayed put, Lewis ignited the flash and opened the shutter. When the flash powder went off—in a small explosion—it sometimes showered sparks over everyone! Lewis had never used a camera before becoming a school photographer: "I'd never taken a picture in my life, much less shot off flash guns. What amazed me was that I didn't blow the town up." Photography was so uncommon at the time that many of the people Lewis photographed had never had their picture taken before. Lewis called his photographs "Hineographs."

Discrimination and Bias in the Early Twentieth Century

All people hold biases, and Lewis Hine was no exception. In some of his articles he expressed beliefs common at the time about the "gentler" roles that women and girls should play in society. We do not know much about his thoughts on race and racism, but he took fewer pictures of Black children than he did of white children. At first, the NCLC focused its efforts on white children, even though Black children often worked under worse conditions. Many of the factories Lewis visited segregated or refused to hire Black workers. Lewis documented some of the injustices he witnessed, such as seventy-five Black sixth graders crowded into a single classroom. He also noted signs of progress, such as glassworkers working side by side, regardless of race. We know that Lewis sought to change the minds of U.S. citizens who were nervous about immigrants and their perceived differences. Although some photographers took pictures from high up or at a distance—making immigrants appear shadowy and far away—Lewis photographed everyone up close and at eye level, with respect. He photographed immigrants from Europe and from Central and South America. He took very few pictures of Asian immigrants or Asian Americans, possibly related to how little time he spent on the West Coast and to racist national policies that prevented or severely limited immigration from many Asian countries in the late nineteenth and early twentieth centuries.

Art for Social Change

Lewis Hine used pictures to bring attention to a problem, and he helped change people's lives. You can find examples of art inspiring social change around the world. The AIDS Memorial Quilt began in 1987 as a way to educate people about HIV and AIDS. It was displayed on the

National Mall in Washington, DC, and today it contains more than forty-eight thousand handmade panels and weighs almost fifty-five tons. In Berlin, Germany, Ai Weiwei created an art installation using fourteen thousand life jackets to raise awareness about the plight of refugees. Many people have created artworks to support the Black Lives Matter movement, making paintings, posters, clothing, street murals, and more. How would you use art to make people pay attention to something important?

LEFT: *Seventy-Five Black Sixth-Grade Children Crowded into One Small Classroom in an Old Store Building, with a Single Teacher, Muskogee, Oklahoma, 1917.*

ABOVE: *Jewish Family Working on Garters in a Kitchen, New York, New York, 1912.*

Time Line: The Life of Lewis Hine and Child Labor in the United States

1874: Lewis Wickes Hine is born on September 26 in Oshkosh, Wisconsin, to parents Sarah Hayes and Douglas Hull Hine. He has two older sisters, Lizzie and Lola. Douglas runs a restaurant serving such dishes as oysters, ham and eggs, pickled pigs' feet, and lemon sherbet.

1889: Douglas Hine suffers poor health and closes the restaurant. Lewis, now fifteen, works as an upholsterer in a furniture factory. "In winter he walked a mile to work, across river ice. He stood freezing … as the wind poured through cracks in the wall. He carried loads too heavy for his years and deficient diet."

LEFT: Lewis as a small child, ca. 1876.

ABOVE RIGHT: *Solution of the Aerial Problem*, drawing by Lewis Hine, 1898.

1889: Florence Kelley publishes a pamphlet, "Our Toiling Children," about the problem of widespread child labor.

1892: Lewis's father, Douglas Hull Hine, dies, reportedly from accidentally shooting himself while cleaning an old revolver.

1893: An economic depression closes the furniture factory. Lewis finds odd jobs like splitting firewood, making deliveries, and selling water filters door to door.

1895: Lewis gains steady employment as a janitor at a bank and continues his studies at night.

1898: As a young man, Lewis dreams of becoming an artist. He illustrates a book of poems that contains one poem for every day of the year; he also carves wood sculptures.

1899: Lewis meets Frank Manny, principal of the Oshkosh State Normal School, who encourages him to get a teaching degree. With Manny's help, Lewis secures a part-time job at the Normal School and begins his studies there.

1900: Lewis enrolls at the University of Chicago and works there to help pay for classes.

1900: U.S. Census shows more than 1.75 million working children between the ages of ten and fifteen.

1901: Manny hires Lewis to teach nature study and geography at the Ethical Culture School in New York, where Manny is now superintendent. Lewis earns a reputation among his students as a great actor. He also enrolls in New York University's School of Education.

1902: Sarah Hayes Hine, Lewis's mother, comes down with a sudden illness. Lewis travels from New York to Wisconsin and arrives at her bedside two hours before she dies.

1903: Mary Harris "Mother" Jones organizes a march of mill children to the home of President Theodore Roosevelt that draws attention to the issue of child labor.

1904: Lewis marries Sarah Ann Rich on August 24. Manny appoints Lewis as school photographer. Lewis learns to use a camera along with his students. He takes pictures of school life and brings his students on trips to Ellis Island to photograph immigrants arriving in the United States.

1904: National Child Labor Committee (NCLC) is established with a mission of "promoting the rights, awareness, dignity, well-being, and education of children and youth as they relate to work and working."

1905: Lewis receives a master of pedagogy degree from New York University. He starts a school photography club.

1906–7: Lewis publishes his first articles about photography. He accepts freelance jobs, including taking pictures for the NCLC.

1908: Lewis leaves teaching and becomes an investigative photographer for the NCLC.

1908–17: Lewis's pictures help arouse nationwide public support and pave the way for child labor reform.

1909: Lewis produces more than eight hundred photographs in one year. He hires an assistant to develop his pictures in the darkroom. Lewis's photos appear in newspapers, pamphlets, posters, and illustrated lectures. He prepares exhibits to reach as many people as possible. He purchases new equipment, possibly including the Graflex camera he would use for most of his career.

1911: By now, thirty states have raised the minimum age for child labor. Many have passed new laws keeping kids in school longer and limiting working hours.

1912: U.S. government establishes the Children's Bureau to "investigate and report…upon all matters pertaining to the welfare of children," including working conditions.

1912: On December 8, Lewis and Sarah have a son, Corydon. The Hines purchase land in Hastings-on-Hudson, New York, for a future home.

1916: Congress passes the Keating-Owen Act, which limits work hours and is the first national law banning the interstate sale of goods produced with child labor.

1916–17: Lewis travels across the country to photograph children working, and he takes detailed notes about each child he meets. This year alone he travels more than fifty thousand miles.

ABOVE LEFT: *An Immigrant Mother and Child, Ellis Island, New York, 1908.*

ABOVE: *Sarah Rich Hine and Corydon Hine, New York, New York, 1915–16.*

1917–18: Lewis and his family move to the home they've built in Hastings-on-Hudson. The top floor of the house is used by a local progressive school.

1918: Lewis leaves the NCLC and joins the American Red Cross. He travels throughout Europe to document Red Cross relief efforts during and after World War I.

1918: U.S. Supreme Court overturns the Keating-Owen Act.

1919: Lewis returns to New York.

1919: Congress enacts the Child Labor Tax Law, which uses taxes to regulate child labor.

1920s: Lewis begins a series of what he calls "work portraits," celebrating skilled laborers and unsung workers as more and more machines enter the workplace.

1922: U.S. Supreme Court overturns the Child Labor Tax Law.

1924: The Art Directors Club of New York awards Lewis its prize for photography.

1924: U.S. Senate adopts the Child Labor Amendment to the U.S. Constitution and sends it to states for ratification. Twenty-eight states ratify it by 1937. Technically, it is still open to states for ratification today.

1930: Lewis photographs the construction of the Empire State Building in New York City. He balances in a basket one hundred stories up to capture the dangerous work of the "sky boys" building the new landmark.

1932: Lewis publishes *Men at Work*, a book for young adults, featuring his work portraits. He dedicates the book to Frank Manny.

Mid- to late 1930s: During the Great Depression, Lewis struggles to find work. He picks up some photography jobs but has a hard time making a living.

1938: Congress passes the Fair Labor Standards Act, establishing minimum age limits, restricting working hours, creating a minimum wage, and ensuring safe workplace conditions for young people.

ABOVE: *Workers Constructing the Empire State Building, New York, New York*, 1931.

LEFT: *Black Steel Worker at Baldwin Locomotive Works, Eddystone, Pennsylvania*, 1937.

1939: A retrospective exhibition of Lewis's photography is held at the Riverside Museum in New York. Sarah Rich Hine, Lewis's wife, dies of pneumonia on Christmas morning, three days before her sixty-fifth birthday.

1940: Lewis Wickes Hine dies on November 4, at age sixty-six. Corydon donates his father's photographs and plates to the Photo League, and later they are donated to George Eastman House. The NCLC eventually gives 5,100 of Lewis's photographs and 355 glass negatives to the U.S. Library of Congress. Others of Lewis's many photographs find homes in museums around the world, including the J. Paul Getty Museum in Los Angeles.

1941: U.S. Supreme Court upholds the Fair Labor Standards Act; a lasting federal law is finally in place.

1985–2014: The NCLC grants annual Lewis Hine Awards for Service to Children and Youth to honor individuals dedicated to helping young people.

ABOVE TOP:
Breaker Boys at the Pennsylvania Coal Company, South Pittston, Pennsylvania, 1911.

ABOVE: *Boys on Their Lunch Break from the Brown Shoe Factory, Moberly, Missouri,* 1910.

Selected Sources

Bengali, Shashank, and Zulfiqar Ali. "How Coronavirus Could Wipe Out Two Decades of Progress in the War against Child Labor." *Los Angeles Times*, June 30, 2020. https://www.latimes.com/world-nation/story/2020-06-30/child-labor-rising-again-in-covid-19-pandemic.

Fliter, John A. "Chronology of Events." In *Child Labor in America: The Epic Legal Struggle to Protect Children*, 241–46. Lawrence: University Press of Kansas, 2018. https://doi.org/10.2307/j.ctv7hot22.14.

Freedman, Russell. *Kids at Work: Lewis Hine and the Crusade against Child Labor*. New York: Clarion Books, 1994.

Goldberg, Vicki. *Lewis W. Hine: Children at Work*. Munich: Prestel, 1999.

Gutman, Judith Mara, and International Fund for Concerned Photography. *Lewis W. Hine: Two Perspectives*. Vol. 4 of *ICP Library of Photographers*. New York: Grossman, 1974.

Hine, Lewis. *America & Lewis Hine: Photographs 1904–1940*. With contributions by Naomi Rosenblum, Walter Rosenblum, and Alan Trachtenberg. Millerton, NY: Aperture, 1977.

Hine, Lewis W., for the National Child Labor Committee. "Baltimore to Biloxi and Back: The Child's Burden in Oyster and Shrimp Canneries." *Survey* 30, no. 5 (May 3, 1913): 167–72.

Hine, Lewis Wickes. *Men at Work: Photographic Studies of Modern Men and Machines*. 2nd ed. New York: Dover, 1977.

J. Paul Getty Museum. "Lewis W. Hine." Museum Collection. http://www.getty.edu/art/collection/artists/1566/lewis-w-hine-american-1874-1940/.

Kaplan, Dail, ed. *Photo Story: Selected Letters and Photographs of Lewis W. Hine*. Washington, DC: Smithsonian Institution Press, 1992.

Library of Congress. "National Child Labor Committee Collection." Digital Collection. https://www.loc.gov/collections/national-child-labor-committee/about-this-collection/.

Macieski, Robert. *Picturing Class: Lewis W. Hine Photographs Child Labor in New England*. Amherst: University of Massachusetts Press, 2015.

Maki, Reid. "Timeline of Child Labor Developments in the United States." *Stop Child Labor*, October 20, 2010. http://stopchildlabor.org/?p=1795.

Marks, Robert W. "Portrait of Lewis Hine." *Coronet* 5, no. 4 (February, 1939): 147–57.

Nemerov, Alexander. *Soulmaker: The Times of Lewis Hine*. Princeton, NJ: Princeton University Press, 2016.

Pérez-Peña, Richard. "Futures in Peril: The Rise of Child Labor in the Pandemic." *New York Times*, September 27, 2020. https://www.nytimes.com/2020/09/27/world/asia/coronavirus-education-child-labor.html.

Sampsell-Willmann, Kate. *Lewis Hine as Social Critic*. Jackson: University Press of Mississippi, 2009.

Trachtenberg, Alan. "Camera/Social Work." In *Reading American Photographs: Images as History; Mathew Brady to Walker Evans*, 164–230. New York: Hill & Wang, 1989.

Whoriskey, Peter, and Rachel Siegel. "Cocoa's Child Laborers." *Washington Post*, June 5, 2019. https://www.washingtonpost.com/graphics/2019/business/hershey-nestle-mars-chocolate-child-labor-west-africa/.

Quotations

"There were two things…": Lewis Hine (LH) as quoted in Marks, "Portrait of Lewis Hine," 157.

"If I could tell…": LH to Paul Kellogg, Aug. 14, 1922, in Kaplan, ed., *Photo Story*, 26.

"A heavy load…": LH to Elizabeth McCausland, Oct. 23, 1938, in Kaplan, *Photo Story*, 126.

"The human spirit…": LH to Florence Kellogg, Feb. 17, 1933, in Kaplan, *Photo Story*, 49.

"Come out with me…", **"Boys and girls…"**, and **"Minute upon minute…"**: LH, "Baltimore to Biloxi and Back," *Survey*, 169, 170, 171.

"At first…": LH, "Children or Cotton? Raising the Question of Cotton Picking in Texas," *Survey* 31, no. 19 (February, 1914): 589.

"Whatta pal! (Watta pal!)": LH to Roy Stryker, Dec. 5, 1938, in Kaplan, *Photo Story*, 139.

*****"Waterproof nonsinkable reasons…"**: LH to Elizabeth McCausland, Oct. 25, 1938, in Kaplan, *Photo Story*, 128.

"I don't remember…": LH, December 1908, photographic print, Library of Congress, Washington, DC, https://www.loc.gov/pictures/item/2018674747/.

"The coal…": LH, "Mr. Coal's Story," *Child Labor Bulletin* 2 (1913–14): 38.

"Up again…": LH to Frank Manny, May 2, 1910, in Kaplan *Photo Story*, 5.

"Stanley is afraid…": LH, May 1910, photographic print, Library of Congress, Washington, DC, https://www.loc.gov/pictures/item/2018674614/.

"Three years…": LH, January 1913, photographic print, Library of Congress, Washington, DC, https://www.loc.gov/pictures/item/2018674796/.

"Hineographs": LH to "Vic and Paul," Dec. 7, 1938, in Kaplan, *Photo Story*, 141.

*****"Perhaps you are weary…"**: LH, "Social Photography: How the Camera May Help in the Social Uplift." In *Proceedings of the National Conference of Charities and Correction* (Fort Wayne, IN: Press of Fort Wayne, 1909), 357.

"Flimsy and unreliable…": LH to Elizabeth McCausland, October 23, 1938, in Kaplan, *Photo Story*, 126.

"I'd never taken…": LH as quoted in Marks, "Portrait of Lewis Hine," 151.

"In winter…": Marks, "Portrait of Lewis Hine," 147.

*Some words were omitted from the original quotation.

ABOVE LEFT: *Edgar Kitchen, Thirteen Years Old, Bowling Green, Kentucky, 1916.*

LEFT: *Woman and Her Children, Nine and Six Years Old, Work at Flower Making, New York, New York, 1915.*

ABOVE: *Five-Year-Old Helen and Her Stepsisters Hulling Strawberries, Seaford, Delaware, 1910.*

Dedicated to my father, a photographer in his own right, and to Bill Reese, who introduced me to Lewis Hine. Thank you for everything. ASDH

Dedicated to our daughter Alice Garland. MG

© 2021 J. Paul Getty Trust

Text © Alexandra S. D. Hinrichs
Illustrations © Michael Garland

Published by Getty Publications, Los Angeles
1200 Getty Center Drive, Suite 500
Los Angeles, California 90049-1682
getty.edu/publications

Elizabeth S. G. Nicholson, *Project Editor*
Amanda Sparrow, *Copy Editor*
Jim Drobka, *Designer*
Michelle Deemer and Molly McGeehan, *Production*
Kelly Peyton, *Image and Rights Acquisition*

Distributed in North America by ABRAMS, New York

Distributed outside North America by Yale University Press, London

Printed in China by Wai Man Book Binding
First printing by Getty Publications

Library of Congress Cataloging-in-Publication Data

Names: Hinrichs, Alexandra S. D., 1984– author. | Garland, Michael, 1952– illustrator. | Getty Publications, issuing body.
Title: The traveling camera : Lewis Hine and the fight to end child labor / by Alexandra S. D. Hinrichs ; illustrated by Michael Garland.
Description: First edition. | Los Angeles, California : Getty Publications, 2021. | Includes bibliographical references. | Audience: Ages 6 and up | Audience: Grades K–5 | Summary: "This biographic picture book chronicles Lewis Hine's effort to end child labor in the US in the early 20th century through his work as a photographer for the National Child Labor Committee (NCLC)"—Provided by publisher.
Identifiers: LCCN 2020043102 | ISBN 9781947440067 (hardcover)
Subjects: LCSH: Hine, Lewis Wickes, 1874–1940—Juvenile literature. | Photographers—United States—Biography—Juvenile literature. | Child labor—United States—Juvenile literature. | LCGFT: Biographies. | Picture books.
Classification: LCC TR140.H52 H56 2021 | DDC 770.92 [B]—dc23
LC record available at https://lccn.loc.gov/2020043102

Illustration Credits
Every effort has been made to contact the owners and photographers of illustrations reproduced here whose names do not appear in the captions or in the illustration credits listed below. Anyone having further information concerning copyright holders is asked to contact Getty Publications so this information can be included in future printings.

p. 1, O. J. Rader, *Lewis Hine,* ca. 1905, digital positive from original gelatin silver negative, 1985.0303.0082 and **p. 35,** Horton and Spink, Lewis Hine as a child, ca. 1876, 1978.1059.0059: Courtesy of the George Eastman Museum; **p. 27,** *Route Boys,* **p. 29,** *Roland, Messenger Boys, Manuel,* **p. 32,** *Minnie,* **p. 33,** *Boys Working,* **p. 34,** *Seventy-Five Children, Jewish Family,* **p. 38,** *Breaker Boys,* **p. 39,** *Edgar Kitchen, Woman and Her Children, Five-Year-Old Helen,* **p. 40,** *Seven-Year-Old Rosie, Boy Working,* and **p. 41,** *Dinner-Toters, Midnight, Selling Vegetables:* Library of Congress, Prints and Photographs Division, National Child Labor Committee Collection; **p. 27,** *Five Messengers,* **p. 29,** *Millie, Sadie, Three Coalminers,* **p. 32,** *Ten-Year-Old Picker, Two Girls,* **p. 36,** *An Immigrant Mother,* **p. 37,** *Workers Constructing, Black Steel Worker,* **p. 38,** *Boys on Lunch Break,* **p. 40,** *Pin Boys,* and **p. 41,** Lewis photographing newsie: J. Paul Getty Museum; **p. 33,** Lewis using box camera, 1906–7, P1981.1.6, **p. 35,** Lewis Hine, *Solution of the Aerial Problem,* 1898, 6914-80, and **p. 36,** Sarah Rich Hine and Corydon: Courtesy of the Oshkosh Public Museum, Oshkosh, WI.